S0-DTC-623

PURNELL

SBN 361 02952 7
© 1974 Purnell & Sons Ltd.
Made and printed in Great Britain by
Purnell & Sons Ltd., Paulton (Somerset) and London
First published 1974 by Purnell Books, Berkshire House,
Queen Street, Maidenhead, Berkshire.

My First Colour Library

Animal Babies

by Jane Carruth

Illustrated by
John Francis

Lamb

Baby lambs are born in the Spring. The lamb
in this picture has a warm woolly coat.

Fawn

A baby deer is called
a fawn. This shy
little fawn is still
wobbly on his legs.

Foal

A baby horse is called a foal. This gentle foal stays next to her mother.

Her mother is called a mare. She
will take care of her until she is
much bigger.

Chicks

Mother Hen is proud of her family of baby chicks. They are very soft and fluffy.

"Peep! Peep!" They will soon let her know when they are beginning to feel hungry.

Joey

Do you know that a baby
kangaroo is called a Joey?
Joey's home is in
Australia.

Tiger cub

Here is a handsome little tiger cub. He lives in
the jungle where it is ever so hot.

Zebra

Baby Zebra is striped like his mother. He lives in a sunny land called Africa. When zebras are frightened they do not neigh like horses. They bark like dogs!

Elephant

Where is Mummy? This little elephant
wants Mummy to give him a bath
in the river!

Giraffe

When this baby giraffe grows up he will be the tallest animal in the whole world.

Puppy

Have you got a puppy of your own? Perhaps this puppy is dreaming of the bone he buried! There are all kinds of puppies. The one in the picture, with his long ears, is a spaniel.

Calf

The farmer is always very pleased when one of his cows has a calf like the one you see here.

Kid

This baby goat is called a kid. He has a huge appetite and will eat almost anything.

Kitten

If you have a kitten like this one, be sure to play with him and never pull his tail!

Lion cub

Baby lions are called cubs. They are just like kittens when they romp and play.

Ducklings

There are all kinds of ducks. Some are wild and others live on the farm.
Father Duck and his pretty ducklings in the picture are wild ducks out for a swim.

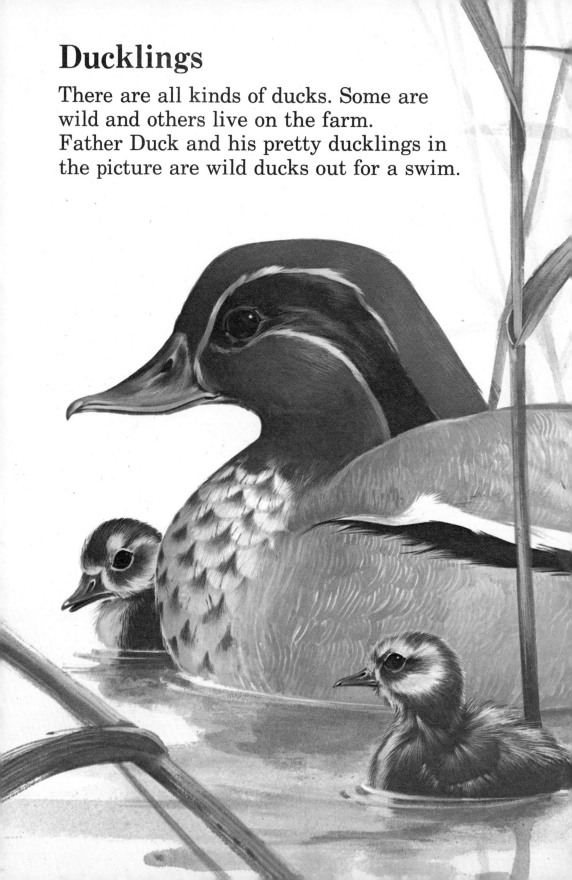

Piglet

Here is Mother Pig, feeding her hungry babies.
Baby pigs are called piglets. Don't you
think their curly tails are funny?

Mother Pig and all her piglets belong to a farmer. He keeps them in their own house, called a sty.

Owl

This is a baby owl. His
big eyes help him to see
in the dark when he goes
hunting.

Fox

Poor baby fox! He has lost his mother. Where can she be? She may be in the den.

Rabbits

Baby rabbits like to play in the sunshine.
But their home is underground in a burrow.

Rabbits are easily frightened. When they
hear a noise they hide in their burrows.

Donkey

Would you like this baby donkey for your own? He will love you if you give him a carrot.

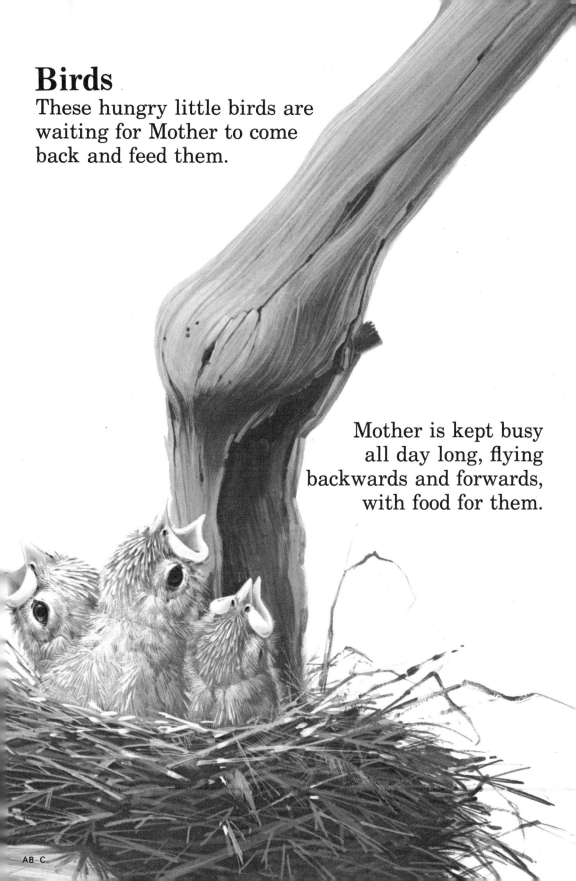

Birds

These hungry little birds are waiting for Mother to come back and feed them.

Mother is kept busy all day long, flying backwards and forwards, with food for them.

Polar bear

This polar bear cub has a lovely
thick, white, furry coat to keep
him nice and warm. Polar bears
live in the coldest parts of the
world amongst all the snow
and ice.

Koala bear

Baby keeps close to Mummy
in his tree home. He has
soft fur, big ears and a
black nose.

Seal pup

Baby seals are called pups. They soon learn to swim and catch fish for their dinner.

Penguins

Penguins are birds, but they can't fly.
They eat fish and they love the water.

Mother Penguin is a great swimmer. She
can swim underwater just as fast
as a seal.

Panda

This baby panda is so pretty that toys are made to look like him. He lives in China.

There are not very many pandas in the world. In their forest home they eat bamboo shoots.

Chimpanzee

Chimpanzees can always make you
laugh at the zoo. Here is Baby showing off.

Dormouse

Tiny baby
Dormouse has
huge eyes. He
hides away in
hedges and is
very shy.

Bear cub

Baby bears are called cubs. They are very playful and, of course, they love honey.

Camel

When this baby camel grows up he will carry his master across the dry, sandy desert.